Bubbles in the sky

"Grandad!" said Max.

"Come and see my bubbles."

"My bubbles are going up."

"Oh, no!

My bubbles are on the fence."

"Oh, no!

My bubbles are on the house."

"Oh, no!

My bubbles are on the shed."

"My bubbles are going up."

"My bubbles are going

up and up."

"My bubbles are going

up to the sky."